Allison Nicoll

Sew It!

Make 17 Projects with Yummy Precut Fabric

Jelly Rolls, Layer Cakes, Charm Packs & Fat Quarters

FunStitch
STUDIO
stitch your art out.

Publisher: Amy Marson

Creative Director: Gailen Runge

Art Director / Book Designer: Kristy Zacharias

Editor: Lynn Koolish

Technical Editors: Susan Nelsen and
Susan Hendrickson

Production Coordinator: Jenny Davis

Production Editor: Katie Van Amburg

Illustrator: Valyrie Gillum

Photo Assistant: Mary Peyton Peppo

Styled photos by Nissa Brehmer, unless otherwise
noted; Instructional photos by Diane Pedersen,
unless otherwise noted

Published by FunStitch Studio, an imprint of C&T Publishing, Inc., P.O. Box 1456, Lafayette, CA 94549

Library of Congress Cataloging-in-Publication Data

Nicoll, Allison, 1981- author.

 Sew it! : make 17 projects with yummy precut fabric--jelly rolls, layer cakes, charm packs & fat quarters /
Allison Nicoll.

   pages cm

ISBN 978-1-60705-874-8 (soft cover)

1. Sewing--Juvenile literature. 2. Textile crafts--Juvenile literature. 3. Patchwork--Patterns--Juvenile
literature. I. Title.

TT712.N53 2014

746--dc23

                    2013042141

Printed in China

10 9 8 7 6 5 4 3 2 1

Dedication

This book is lovingly dedicated to my three gorgeous boys. Riley, Jacob, and Elijah: You are my greatest achievements, and I am so thankful to be your mumma.

Photo by Liz Crocombe, Cutie Patootie Photographie

Acknowledgments

I would like to thank my wonderful husband, Matt: You have always encouraged me to follow my dreams, no matter what. Your support during this season has meant the world to me. Thank you for understanding when I had to meet deadlines, and getting takeout on your way home.

To my beautiful friend Jody: "Thank you" just doesn't seem enough. You have always been my biggest supporter—your love and encouragement have made me believe anything is possible if I work hard enough.

To the wonderful team at C&T Publishing, particularly my editor, Lynn Koolish: Thank you for making my dream become a reality. I have been so blessed to work with an amazing team.

Contents

Let Me Introduce Myself

Hi! I'm Ally. I live in Australia and I teach kids how to sew.

I wrote this book to share my love of stitching with the world—it has seventeen projects that are perfect for kids who want to learn to sew.

Be sure you read the instructions and also the information in the "basics" sections—doing this will make your end results fantastic. Then have a look through the book, pick out your favorite projects, and get sewing!

If you have any questions or want to share pics of your finished projects, I'd love to hear from you—you can email me at ally@quiltingmumma.com or find me on Facebook at facebook.com/quiltingmumma.

I hope this book inspires a love of stitching that will last a lifetime!

Happy stitching!

Ally

Sewing with Precuts

What Are Precuts?

As the name suggests, precuts are fabrics that have been cut to specific sizes and are then sold in bundles.

The projects in this book are made mostly from precut fabrics so you can get to the sewing without a lot of cutting.

Types of Precuts

There are four types of precuts that you can find in quilt and craft stores and online.

2½"-Wide Strips

Strips that are 2½" wide and about 40" long can be used for many projects. About 40 of them are often rolled together. Some of the names for these precut bundles are **Jelly Rolls**, **Rolie Polies**, and **Bali Pops**.

5" × 5" Squares

Precut 5" × 5" squares are also known as charm squares. When about 40 or 42 squares are bundled together, they are sometimes called **Charm Packs** or **5" Stackers**.

10" × 10" Squares

Precut 10" × 10" squares are stacked and tied together, with about 40 or 42 squares per stack. Some of the names for these precut bundles are **Layer Cakes** and **10" Stackers**.

Fat Quarters

A **fat quarter** is a piece of fabric that is 18" × 22". Fat quarters are often sold in bundles, but you can also buy them individually from any good quilting or craft store.

Why Use Precuts?

- **Save money**—You can usually find precuts at a good price, and there is very little waste at the end of your project.

- **Get a variety of fabrics**—Precut packs include lots of different fabrics that are designed to go with each other. You don't have to worry about picking individual fabrics.

- **Save time**—Because precuts are already cut into strips or squares, you spend less time cutting before you begin your project.

As you'll see, precuts can be used in so many sewing projects, from quilts to bags and everything in between!

I love them because they can be used in many ways and are a fantastic value for the money. Besides, who can resist a beautifully wrapped bundle of fabric? Not me.

How to Use This Book

The book is divided into sections by type of precut. Within the sections are projects for every skill level:

1

Starter
Perfect for when you are just starting out. Make these projects first.

2

Next Step
After you've made the Starters, you'll be ready for these projects.

3

Use Your Skills
After you've done some sewing and quilting, take on these projects.

If you are new to sewing or quilting, don't worry. This book was written with you in mind. Everything you need to know is included in this book:

• Getting started: tools and supplies

• Basic skills

• Turning a quilt top into a quilt

Just be sure to read through all the notes and instructions before starting each project and check with an adult if there is anything you are unsure about.

Don't worry about making everything perfect—this is about learning and having fun.

So, what are you waiting for?

Getting Started

Tools & Supplies

Setting Up Your Sewing Area

When you sew and quilt, it's important to have things set up so you are comfortable and have everything you need handy.

- Put the sewing machine on a sturdy table that is the right height for you. If the machine is too high, you'll be uncomfortable and won't be able to do your best work.

- It's best if the machine is set into a sewing table or has an extension table that gives you a flat surface for sewing and quilting.

- Make sure there is good light so you can see what you are doing.

- Have a wastebasket nearby for scraps of fabric and thread so you can keep your sewing area neat.

- Organize all your sewing and quilting tools so you can reach them when you need them.

Sewing Machine

The first thing you need is a sewing machine.

It doesn't matter if you are sewing on a brand-new shiny sewing machine or on an old machine that your grandmother used. As long as the machine runs smoothly, you can use it to make the projects in this book. If the machine hasn't been used in a while, you'll probably want to take it to a sewing machine store to have it cleaned and serviced.

If you've never used a sewing machine before or don't know how to use the machine that you have, find someone who can show you how to use it. Keep the sewing machine manual handy because if you don't know how something on the machine works, you'll want to look it up in the manual.

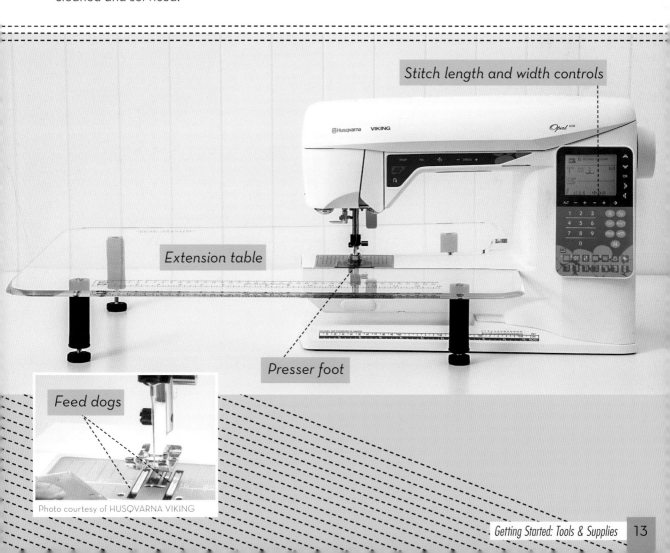

Stitch length and width controls

Extension table

Presser foot

Feed dogs

Photo courtesy of HUSQVARNA VIKING

Sewing Machine Feet

Sewing machine feet walk on top of your fabric. Just kidding! They hold the fabric down while you're sewing. Below the presser foot, you'll see two or three thin metal bars with sharp teeth called feed dogs. As you stitch, the feed dogs move or "feed" the fabric.

Quilts and quilted projects are made with a ¼" seam allowance. This means that your stitching is ¼" from the edge of the fabric.

It's easiest to sew a ¼" seam allowance with a **¼" presser foot**, sometimes called a *patchwork foot*. If you don't have a ¼" foot for your machine, you can get one from your local sewing machine dealer or at a quilting store.

There are two other sewing machine feet that you should think about.

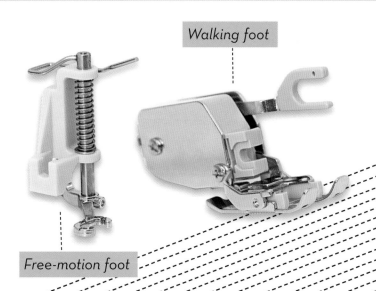

Walking foot

Free-motion foot

- A **walking foot** is a special foot that moves the top fabric along at the same rate as the feed dogs move the bottom fabric. It is particularly helpful when you are quilting.

- If you are going to do free-motion quilting (page 32), you will need a **free-motion foot**, sometimes called a *darning* foot or a *hopping* foot (because it moves up and down).

Sewing Machine Needles

There are many different types of needles that can be used in a sewing machine. Using the correct needle really does make a difference. Using the wrong needle type or size can ruin a project. A **topstitch needle** is a good all-purpose needle, and size 90/14 is just the right size for the projects in this book.

Needles get dull from stitching, so it is important to put in a new needle after you have been sewing for about 8–10 hours.

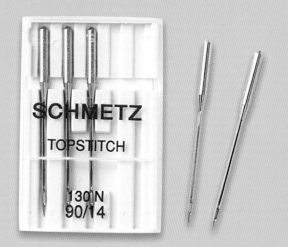

------ *Try This Now* ------

This is a good time to sit down and practice using your machine. You'll need some thread, some fabric, and scissors. Here are the things you should know how to do:

- *Thread the machine.*

- *Wind a bobbin.*

- *Sew forward and backward (backstitch).*

- *Sew with a ¼" seam allowance.*

If you don't know how to do any of these things, have someone show you or look at the sewing machine manual to learn how.

--*TIP*---

Sewing is much more fun when the sewing machine runs smoothly. If your machine skips stitches or keeps breaking the thread, you'll have a hard time sewing. To keep these problems from happening, be sure that your machine is serviced at least once a year.

Cutting Tools

Quilting involves cutting, even when you are using precuts. Cutting can be done with a rotary cutter or with scissors.

Rotary Cutting Tools

Quilters often use rotary cutters, acrylic rulers, and cutting mats to cut their fabric.

A **rotary cutter** is a very, very sharp round blade in a handle that must always be used very carefully. If you aren't comfortable using a rotary cutter, use scissors instead. There isn't a lot of cutting in this book, so using scissors isn't a big deal.

The **acrylic rulers** that are used with rotary cutters come in many sizes and shapes. You use the grid on the ruler to make sure the ruler is lined up with the fabric to cut straight and even. A good ruler to start with is 6½" × 24". This size allows you to cut or draw a line the entire width of the fabric.

If you use a rotary cutter, you must use a **rotary cutting mat**. These flexible mats have lines on them to help you keep your fabric straight.

Scissors

Even if you have a rotary cutter, you should have three types of scissors:

Good fabric shears in a size that fits your hand (don't cut anything that isn't fabric with these scissors)

Little scissors or snips to cut thread when you are sewing

All-purpose scissors for cutting everything that isn't fabric

Safety Alert!

If you are going to use a rotary cutter, follow these guidelines:

- *Check with a parent before you use a rotary cutter for the first time.*

- *Always follow the Rules for Using a Rotary Cutter (page 20).*

- *Consider wearing a safety glove on your noncutting hand. A source for this glove is listed in Resources (page 127).*

Seam Ripper

We all make mistakes. When you're sewing and quilting, it's best to get it over with and fix mistakes before you move on. The easiest way to take out stitches is to cut every third stitch or so with a **seam ripper** and then pull out the uncut thread from the other side.

Safety Alert!

- *Seam rippers are sharp and it's easy to jab yourself—be careful when using a seam ripper!*

Iron

A good iron is essential for pressing your fabric and seams.

Be sure to keep your iron soleplate (bottom) clean, especially if you do any fusible appliqué. Refer to Appliqué (page 27) for instructions on using paper-backed fusible web. If you do get any fusible on your iron, be sure to clean it off with iron cleaner from a craft or quilt shop.

Safety Alert!

- *Check with a parent before you use an iron for the first time, and learn how it works. Not all irons work the same way.*

- *Irons get extremely hot and can burn you, your fabric, or the ironing board cover if you aren't careful.*

Pins

STRAIGHT PINS

Every sewist needs pins. Glass-headed pins are my favorite and come in many colors and sizes. If you accidentally iron over them, they won't melt.

CURVED SAFETY PINS

When it's time to quilt your projects, you'll need to hold together the top, batting, and backing. Curved safety pins are perfect for the job. Read about basting in Getting Ready to Quilt (page 30).

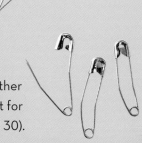

Additional Fabric

In addition to precut fabrics, you may also need fabric for quilt backs, bindings, and so on.

I recommend that you use fabrics that are 100% cotton. It's a good idea to wash, dry, and iron your fabrics before you use them.

When you buy fabric off of the bolt, instead of precut, it is usually 40"–44" wide. It comes folded in half. It's easiest to work with if you keep it folded this way. If you wash your fabric before you use it, fold it in half again, just as it was when you bought it.

Thread

To get good results when you sew, you need to use good thread. Don't use cheap bargain thread because it will shred and break.

You can use cotton thread, polyester thread, or cotton/polyester thread. If you can, get your thread at a quilt or fabric store. You can tell the employees what you are making and they can help you pick out thread that will work for you. It's good to have several spools on hand in various colors to coordinate with your projects.

Batting

Batting is what goes in the middle of the quilt to make it soft and cuddly. Two different types of batting are used for the projects in this book. Both should be available at your local quilt or craft store.

Quilt Batting

There are many different types and brands of batting for quilts. I recommend that you buy what's called an 80/20 blend—80% cotton and 20% polyester. This type of batting is easy to use.

You can buy batting either in packages or by the yard. Either way is fine. Just make sure you have enough for your project. Save the scraps to use for smaller projects.

Fusible Fleece

Fusible fleece is like batting except that it has fusible (iron-on) glue on one side. You iron your fabric to it, and it stays in place—you can quilt it if you like, but you don't need to. The bag and pouch projects in this book use fusible fleece.

When using fusible fleece, be sure to read the instructions that come with it. Different brands have different instructions on how long you need to press it.

Basic Skills

There are a few special skills you'll need in order to make the projects in this book.

Cutting Fabric

Even though you are starting mostly with precut fabric, you (or an adult helping you) will still need to do a little cutting.

Cutting Fabric into Strips with a Rotary Cutter

If you are using a rotary cutter, you will also need a rotary cutting mat and a ruler that is meant to be used with the rotary cutter (see Rotary Cutting Tools, page 16).

Rules for Using a Rotary Cutter

Be sure to follow these rules whenever you are using a rotary cutter:

- Pay attention to what you are doing at all times. One little slip can result in a serious cut.

- Always close or lock the cutter when you are not using it. This means locking it right after you make a cut and unlocking it just before you make a cut.

- When you are cutting, hold the ruler securely and make sure all your fingers are out of the way of the cutter.

- Put the cutter away in a safe place when you are done using it for the day.

When you are making quilts and other projects, it is very important that the edges of your fabric be straight and even. Straight, even edges allow you to cut strips or pieces of fabric that are the same width for the entire length of the strip. And straight, even strips make it easier for you to sew everything together.

1. Place your fabric on a cutting mat with the folded edge closest to you, lined up along a line on the cutting mat. A

2. Line up your ruler as shown, and trim off the uneven edge to the right. B

3. Don't move the fabric edge that you just cut, but make sure all the fabric is on the cutting mat. Turn the mat around so the edge you just cut is now on the left. C

4. Now you are ready to cut strips or pieces.

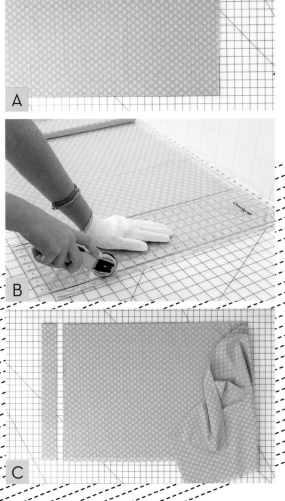

A

B

C

5. Use the lines on the ruler to measure and cut the fabric to the size you need. For example, if you need to cut 2½"-wide strips, line up the edge of the fabric with the 2½" line on the ruler and cut your fabric. D

TIP

After you cut your first strip, unfold it and take a look at it. If it has a V in it or one end of the strip is wider than the other, try the following:

1. *Make sure your fabric is folded evenly.*

2. *Trim any uneven edges.*

3. *Cut another strip and make sure it is okay.*

6. To cut another strip, move the ruler gently along the fabric. Line up the edge of the fabric with the 2½" line on the ruler and cut another strip.

7. If you are cutting a lot of strips, the fabric can shift a bit and your strips might get uneven. So every now and then, turn your fabric around so it looks like it did in Step 1. Make sure it is folded evenly and trim off any uneven edges. Turn the cutting mat around and continue cutting strips.

Cutting Fabric into Strips with Scissors

If you are using scissors instead of a rotary cutter, follow the instructions for rotary cutting, but draw lines and cut on the lines. Be careful to keep the fabric neatly folded as you use the scissors, though.

Crosscutting Strips with a Rotary Cutter

For some of the projects in this book, you will need to crosscut strips into squares or rectangles. To do this, follow these steps.

1. Place a strip on the cutting mat. A

2. Trim off the *selvages.* B

> **SELVAGE:** *The narrow, tightly woven part that is on the edges of the fabric.*

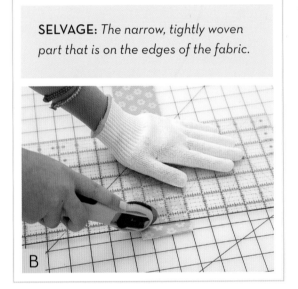

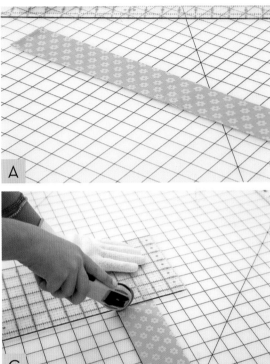

3. Line up the edge of the fabric with the line on the ruler for the size you need. For example, if you have a 2½″-wide strip and you are cutting squares, line up the edge of the fabric with the 2½″ line on the ruler. Then cut along the edge of the ruler. C

4. Repeat to cut as many squares as you need.

-- Try This Now ----------------------------

It's a good idea to practice cutting before you cut into your project fabric. Using a rotary cutter or scissors, try cutting a few long strips and then crosscutting those strips into squares or rectangles.

Pinning and Sewing

Pinning

Pins hold pieces of fabric until you sew them together—they are like extra helping hands. Pin as much as you need, but remember to remove the pins just before you get to them when you are sewing with a sewing machine.

----TIP----------

Don't ever sew over pins—not only will the pins bend and break, but you can break your sewing machine!

Sewing

Most fabric has two sides, a right side and a wrong side. If there is a right side and a wrong side, the right side is the prettier, brighter side. Most of the sewing in this book is done by placing the fabrics *right sides together* and sewing a seam. If the project instructions say "pin and sew," the pieces are sewn with right sides together. Always read the project instructions carefully in case pieces need to be sewn together in a different way.

If you are making a quilt, you will usually sew blocks into rows. When you are sewing lots of blocks together, it can be pretty hard to keep them in order without a trick. Here's a numbering idea for you: Number your blocks, and then sew the rows together.

---COOL TRICK! ---

Numbering Your Blocks

Numbering your blocks is a good way to make sure you sew them together in the right order. Number each row and give each block a letter in the row. Write the numbers on scraps of paper and safety pin them to the blocks.

1A	1B	1C	1D	1E	1F
2A	2B	2C	2D	2E	2F
3A	3B	3C	3D	3E	3F
4A	4B	4C	4D	4E	4F
5A	5B	5C	5D	5E	5F
6A	6B	6C	6D	6E	6F
7A	7B	7C	7D	7E	7F

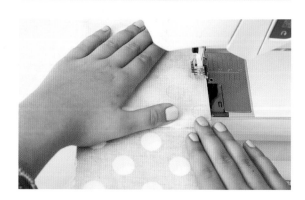

Nesting Seams

When you are sewing blocks into rows, press the odd-row seams to the right and the even-row seams to the left. This trick will make it easier to sew together the rows because the seams will nest, or butt up against each other.

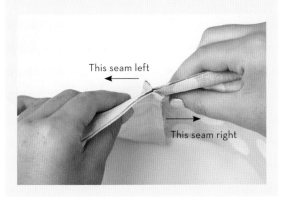

This seam left

This seam right

Go Slowly

I tell my students in class to stitch slowly, just like a snail, because you'll have much better control and accuracy on your project. Go especially slowly as you stitch over seams, where there are multiple layers of fabric. Slowing down will give you a much neater finish. I know it's exciting to start a new project, and you may want to rush ahead. But if you steady yourself and stitch carefully, your end product will be amazing!

Seam Allowances

All seam allowances are ¼" unless another seam allowance size is given. It's important to sew with accurate seam allowances so that your pieces fit together properly. Refer to Sewing Machine Feet (page 14).

I strongly recommend a ¼" foot or patchwork foot for your sewing machine.

Stitch Length

Sewing machines have a screen panel, a knob, or a dial that lets you control how long each stitch is. On some machines it's measured in stitches per inch. On other machines it's the actual stitch length in millimeters.

For piecing and general sewing, use a stitch length of 2–2.5, or 11–14 stitches per inch.

For quilting, you might want to increase the stitch length to 3–3.5, or 8–9 stitches per inch, because longer stitches show up better.

Pressing

I'm sure you'll be surprised to hear that there are a lot of different opinions about pressing. The main item of discussion is whether or not to use steam. I think that either way is fine.

What is most important is that you know the difference between *pressing* and *ironing*. You'll be pressing—that means picking up the iron, pressing down with it, and then picking up the iron again. Ironing is sliding the iron along the fabric. Don't iron, because that can stretch the fabric.

For quilts, seam allowances are usually pressed to one side. Follow the pressing instructions given in the projects.

Refer to Cool Trick! Nesting Seams (page 25) for an easy way to make sure your seams line up when you sew together rows.

Try This Now

With the pieces that you used to practice cutting (from Try This Now, page 23), make a sewing practice piece. Sew the pieces into rows, practicing ¼" seams. Press the seams in alternate directions from row to row. Then sew together the rows, nesting the seams.

Using Fusible Fleece

Fusible fleece is easy to use and adds just the right amount of body to bags and pouches.

Each brand of fusible fleece comes with instructions on how to use it. Be sure to read the instructions to learn how hot the iron should be and how long you need to press to make sure the fleece bonds to the fabric.

1. Take the fusible fleece out of the package and feel both sides—one side should feel smooth and the other should feel a bit bumpy. The bumpy side has the fusible glue on it.

2. After you cut your fabric and fusible fleece to the right sizes, place the fusible fleece on the ironing board with the bumpy (fusible) side facing up.

3. Place the fabric, *right* side up, on top of the fusible fleece so that the fleece will be glued to the *wrong* side of the fabric.

4. Using the heat setting indicated on the package, press the fabric to the fusible fleece. Don't iron, but press, picking up the iron each time you need to move it to a new area of fabric. Be sure to press the entire piece of fabric.

Appliqué

Two projects in this book are appliquéd—a design of cut-out fabric shapes is placed on top of the base fabric and then attached by fusing, sewing, or both.

My favorite appliqué method is to use a paper-backed fusible web such as Wonder-Under. When you buy a paper-backed fusible web, you'll get a sheet of fusible glue on a special backing sheet.

The fusible glue melts when it is pressed with an iron and holds together two pieces of fabric. The paper backing keeps the glue from getting on your iron or ironing board.

Each brand of fusible web comes with instructions on how to use it. Be sure to read the instructions to learn how hot the iron should be and how long you need to press to make sure the fusible web melts.

Here's how to use paper-backed fusible web:

1. Trace the pattern you want to use onto the *paper* side of your fusible web. (All the patterns in this book have been drawn for this method of appliqué.)

2. Cut out each shape ¼"–½" outside the drawn line. A

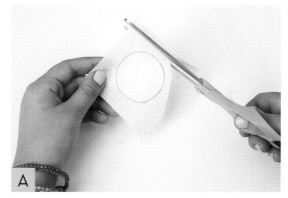

A

3. Place the cut-out shape on the *wrong* side of your chosen fabric, with the paper side facing up. Otherwise you will get the fusible glue on your iron (yuck!). Press the fusible web according to the manufacturer's instructions. The heat will melt the glue just a bit so the fusible glue sticks to the fabric. B

4. Cut along the drawn line of each shape. C

B

C

5. Peel off the paper backing.

6. Place the appliqué right side up on the base fabric and press it in place to permanently attach it.

7. Stitch around the edges of your appliqués to make sure they really stay put. If your sewing machine has a blanket stitch, give it a try. Otherwise you can use a straight stitch.

------- *Try This Now* ------------------------------

Use the patterns for Pretty Flower Pincushion (pages 50 and 51) or Love Hearts Pillow (page 72) to practice fusing. Practice stitching around the edges as well.

Turning a Quilt Top into a Quilt

It's corny, but it's true—when you are making a quilt, it's not a quilt until it's quilted.

Getting Ready to Quilt

The Quilt Sandwich

When you have finished a quilt top, you need to make a *quilt sandwich*. (No, a quilt sandwich isn't a snack to give you energy to turn your quilt top into a quilt.) A quilt sandwich is the quilt top, batting (page 18), and a backing (fabric on the back side of the quilt).

1. For most of the projects in this book, make sure the backing and the batting are 4" larger than your quilt top. For example, if your quilt top is 30" × 35", then you want your quilt backing to be 34" × 39". When you are making larger quilts, you should cut the backing and batting even larger. Follow the instructions given in each project. Press the backing to make sure it is smooth.

2. Place the backing, right side facing down, on a large surface such as a table or hard floor. Smooth it out so there are no wrinkles. Taping the backing to the surface is a good idea to keep the backing smooth.

3. Place the batting on top of the backing, smoothing it out so there are no wrinkles.

4. Place the quilt top in the center of the batting, right side facing up.

Basting

Before you start quilting, you need to *baste* your quilt sandwich. This means holding together the three layers.

The easiest way to do this is with curved safety pins that are made just for basting.

1. Carefully smooth out any wrinkles in the quilt sandwich.

2. Starting in the middle of the quilt, pin together the 3 layers. Use the width of your hand as a guide for spacing the pins.

Quilting

The quilting holds the three layers of the quilt sandwich together. There are several ways to quilt any project.

Straight-line quilting is very easy, even for beginners. With straight-line quilting you sew in straight or very gently curving lines. When you are quilting, make sure that nothing (such as another part of the quilt, the backing, or extra batting) gets folded under the quilt and caught in the quilting.

In-the-ditch quilting is like straight-line quilting, but you stitch in the seamline where the fabric is sewn together. This is called the ditch. It's a little harder than plain straight-line quilting because you need to stitch slowly and carefully to stay in the ditch. You should have a walking foot on your machine. When you are quilting, make sure that nothing (such as another part of the quilt, the backing, or extra batting) gets folded under the quilt and caught in the quilting.

---- TIP ----

You'll have an easier time with straight-line quilting if you have a walking foot on your machine. Refer to Sewing Machine Feet (page 14).

If you need to stop quilting to reposition your hands or move the quilt, or if you just need to take a break, stop with the needle down in the fabric so the quilt won't move when you stop. Some sewing machines even have a needle-down option that you can set.

TIP

Some quilters stitch in-the-ditch before they do their free-motion quilting. The in-the-ditch quilting helps hold everything together.

-- Try This Now

Use your sewing practice piece (from Try This Now, page 26) to practice quilting! Make a few quilt sandwiches (page 30) and try straight lines, gently curving lines, and quilting in-the-ditch.

Free-motion quilting is harder than straight-line quilting but it is lots of fun—you are in complete control! You need to time how fast the machine is stitching with how fast you are moving the quilt. The faster the stitching, the faster you need to move the quilt to have nice stitches. The slower the stitching, the slower you need to move the quilt to have nice stitches.

Before you free-motion quilt, you will need to lower the feed dogs, so refer to your sewing machine manual to do that. Use a special free-motion presser foot, and move the fabric around under the needle. You can go wherever you want—draw pictures or just make lines! When you are quilting, make sure that nothing (such as another part of the quilt, the backing, or extra batting) gets folded under the quilt and caught in the quilting.

Just like in straight-line quilting, if you need to stop quilting to reposition your hands or move the quilt, or if you just need to take a break, stop with the needle down in the fabric so the quilt won't move when you stop. If your sewing machine has a needle-down option, then you can set it.

Free-motion feet are available from stores that sell your brand of sewing machine.

You really want to practice free-motion quilting before you try it on a quilt you've made. Make some quilt sandwiches (page 30) and give it a try. Don't forget to lower the feed dogs. Refer to your sewing machine manual to find out how.

1. Place the quilt sandwich under the needle. Lower the presser foot.

2. Make a frame with your hands.

3. Press on the pedal, and when the needle starts to move, slowly start to move the fabric. Quilt just within the area framed by your hands.

4. When you need to move to another area, stop the machine with the needle down in the fabric. Move your hands to the area you want to quilt next and start quilting again.

Finishing Your Quilt

Trimming

When you are all done with the quilting, you need to trim the extra backing and batting even with the edges of the top. You can do this with scissors or a rotary cutter, ruler, and mat. After trimming everything, it's a good idea to stitch all around the quilt ⅛″ from the outside edge to hold everything securely together. This step will help when you sew on the binding.

The more you practice your free-motion quilting, the better you will get!

Binding

Putting the binding on your quilt finishes the edges. It's like adding a frame and saying the quilt is done!

Binding strips can be different widths, but 2½" is often used. If you have jelly roll strips, they are the right size to use. If you need to cut strips, refer back to Cutting Fabric (page 20).

COOL TRICK!

Binding

The fabric for your binding doesn't have to be all the same—sometimes it's fun to use up leftover fabric to make a scrappy-looking binding.

1. Trim off the *selvages*. A

> **SELVAGE:** *The narrow, tightly woven part that is on the edges of the fabric.*

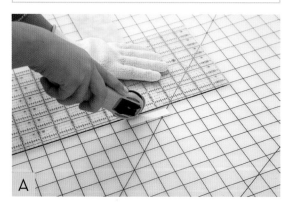

A

2. There is an easy way to sew together the strips so you have enough binding to go all the way around your quilt: Cross the strips as shown and mark a diagonal line from corner to corner with a pencil, and pin. Sew on the drawn line. Trim off the extra fabric, leaving a ¼" seam allowance, and press the seam open. B , C , D

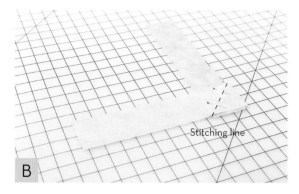

Stitching line

B

C

D

3. Press the strip in half lengthwise with the right sides out. E

4. Starting in the middle of a side, place the binding flat on the front of your quilt with the raw edges aligned. Start sewing about 6" from the end of the binding. A walking foot can be helpful when sewing on the binding. F

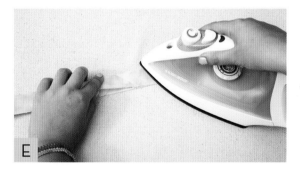

5. Sew until you are ¼" from the corner. Stop stitching and *backstitch*. Cut the thread and take the quilt out from under the presser foot.

BACKSTITCHING: *Stitching backward for a few stitches to keep the seam from coming unstitched.*

---TIP---

The more accurate you are in stopping exactly ¼" from the corner, the better your binding will look. Sew slowly, and as you get close to the corner, stop stitching with the needle down (so the quilt won't shift position). Line up the binding over the corner of the quilt, and place a pin ¼" from the corner so you can see your stopping point.

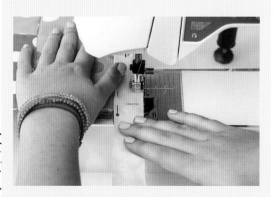

6. Fold the binding up to make a 45° angle. Then fold the binding straight down. There will be a little flap in the corner, which will make the mitered corner in the binding. It helps to pin the binding so it doesn't slip when you start sewing again. G , H , I

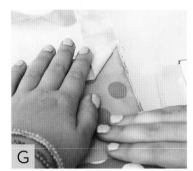

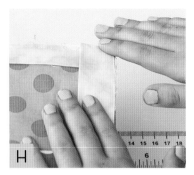

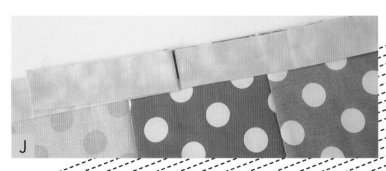

7. Start stitching again and continue to the next corner. Repeat Steps 5, 6, and 7 for each corner.

8. There is a really neat trick to finishing the ends of the binding so you won't even see where you sewed together the ends: Fold the ending tail of the binding back on itself where it meets the beginning binding tail. From the fold, measure and mark 2½" (or the width of your binding strips). Cut the ending binding tail at this mark. J , K

9. Open both tails. Place 1 tail on top of the other tail at right angles, right sides together, and pin. Mark a diagonal line from corner to corner and stitch on the line. Check that you've done it correctly and that the binding fits the quilt. Then trim the seam allowance to ¼". Press the seam allowance open. L

10. Refold the binding and stitch this binding section in place on the quilt. M

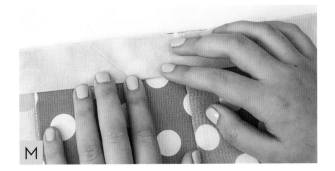

11. Fold the binding to the back of the quilt, covering the raw edges. Use a hand sewing needle to stitch the binding to the back of the quilt. N

Congratulations!
You've finished your quilt!!

Projects

The projects in this book are organized by the type of precut fabric used to make them. The list below shows all the projects by skill level. For example, if you want to start with all the easiest projects first, you can select from the Starter projects. If you've been sewing for a while, you can jump into the Next Step or Use Your Skills projects.

1 Starter projects

Perfect for when you are just starting out. Make these projects first.

Sewing Machine Mat, page 40
(5″ × 5″ squares)

Retro Moments Quilt, page 44
(5″ × 5″ squares)

Pretty Flower Pincushion, page 48
(5″ × 5″ squares)

Sweet Little Pouch, page 58
(10″ × 10″ squares)

Concrete Jungle Quilt, page 80
(2½″ strips)

I Can Sing a Rainbow Quilt, page 86
(2½″ strips)

Striped Pillow, page 92
(2½″ strips)

Sleepover Set—Pillowcase, page 102
(fat quarters)

2 Next Step projects

After you've made the Starters, you'll be ready for these projects.

Wall Organizer, page 52
(5″ × 5″ squares)

Tropicana Quilt, page 62
(10″ × 10″ squares)

Love Hearts Pillow, page 68
(10″ × 10″ squares)

Snowballs Quilt, page 74
(10″ × 10″ squares)

Accessories Pouch, page 96
(2½″ strips)

Shooting Stars Pencil Roll, page 112
(fat quarters)

3 Use Your Skills projects

After you've done some sewing and quilting, take on these projects.

Sleepover Set—Essentials Bag, page 106
(fat quarters)

Day Trip Messenger Bag, page 116
(fat quarters)

Indie Sling Bag, page 122
(fat quarters)

5" × 5" Squares:

Charm Packs
OR 5" Stackers

1 Starter Sewing Machine Mat

If you have a sewing machine, you need a sewing machine mat! The mat is also a great size to use as a placemat. These are so easy that you can make one for everyone in your family.

Here's What You Need

- 15 squares 5" × 5"
- ¼ yard fabric for binding
- ½ yard fabric for backing
- 14" × 23" piece of fusible fleece

Before You Start

- Read through all the instructions before doing any cutting or sewing.

- If you don't know how to do something or you don't remember, go back to that section in the book and find out how.

Here's What to Do

Remember: Seam allowances are ¼".

1. Arrange your 5" × 5" squares into 3 rows of 5 squares each. To keep your blocks in order, refer to Cool Trick! Numbering Your Blocks (page 24) to label your blocks.

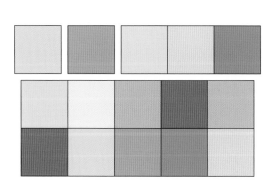

2. Stitch the blocks into rows. Refer to Cool Trick! Nesting Seams (page 25). Press the odd-row seams to the right and the even-row seams to the left.

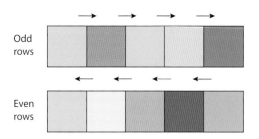

Odd rows

Even rows

3. Stitch together the rows to complete the mat. Give it a good pressing to make sure all the seams are flat and smooth.

4. Press the fusible fleece to the *wrong* side of the pieced mat. Refer to Using Fusible Fleece (page 26).

5. Cut the backing fabric so it is 15″ × 25″. *Note: The backing only needs to be 2″ larger than the pieced top because this project is quite small. Cut 2 strips 2½″ wide from the binding fabric.*

6. Refer to Turning a Quilt Top into a Quilt (page 29) to layer, quilt, and bind your mat. To quilt my mat, I stitched in-the-ditch. *Note: Because you've used fusible fleece, you won't have a separate batting layer.*

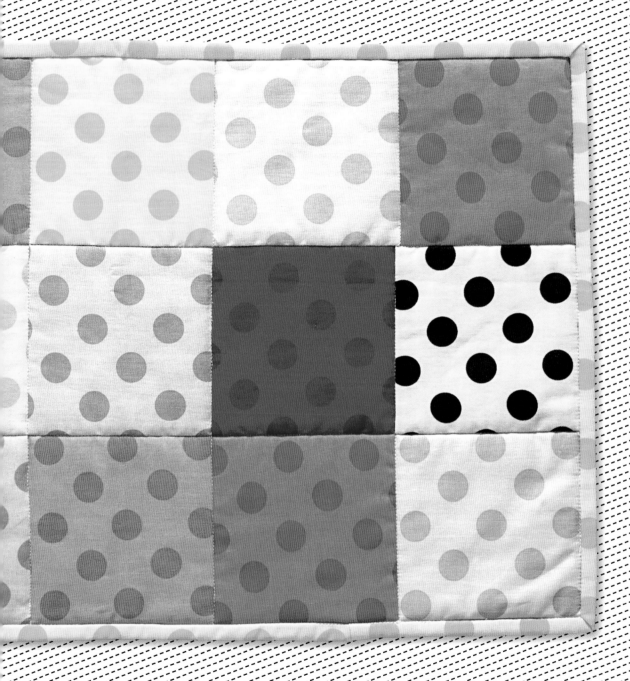

Finished size: 35½" × 40" • Finished block size: 4½" × 4½"

Fabrics used: 2wenty-thr3e by Moda

Starter 1 Retro Moments Quilt

This project is one that is loved by all the new girls who come to my sewing class. It's a great first project, as it gives you a chance to learn many skills that are commonly used in patchwork, including pinning, piecing, and quilting.

Here's What You Need

- 42 squares 5" × 5"
- ¾ yard gray fabric for borders
- ⅜ yard fabric for binding
- 1¼ yards fabric for backing
- 39" × 44" piece of batting

Before You Start

- Read through all the instructions before doing any cutting or sewing.

- If you don't know how to do something or you don't remember, go back to that section in the book and find out how.

Pick fabrics that you love, and this quilt will come together in no time.

Here's What to Do

Remember: Seam allowances are ¼".

Make the Quilt Center

1. Look at the quilt photo (page 47) and the quilt diagram to arrange the 5" × 5" squares in 7 rows with 6 blocks in each row. To keep your blocks in order, refer to Cool Trick! Numbering Your Blocks (page 24) to label your blocks.

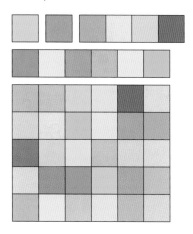

2. Stitch the blocks into rows. Refer to Cool Trick! Nesting Seams (page 25). Press the odd-row seams to the right and the even-row seams to the left.

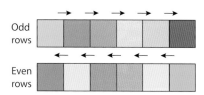

3. Stitch together the rows to complete the quilt top. Give the top a good pressing to make sure all the seams are flat and smooth.

Add the Borders

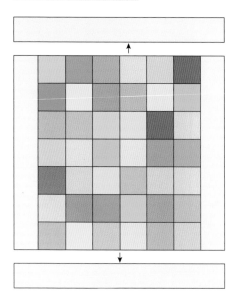

1. Cut 4 strips 4½" wide across the width of your border fabric. Trim 2 of the strips so they are 4½" × 32" for the side borders. Refer to Cutting Fabric (page 20).

2. Look at the side borders in the quilt diagram. Pin and stitch these strips to the sides of your quilt top. Press the seams toward the outside.

3. Cut the remaining 2 border strips so they are 4½" × 35½" for the top and bottom borders.

4. Look at the top and bottom borders in the quilt diagram. Pin and stitch these strips to the top and bottom of your quilt top. Press the seams toward the outside.

Put Together the Quilt

1. Cut the backing fabric to 39" × 44".

2. Assemble your quilt sandwich, baste, and quilt. Refer to Turning a Quilt Top into a Quilt (page 29). I used straight-line and stitch in-the-ditch quilting.

3. Cut 4 strips 2½" wide across the width of the binding fabric. Refer to Finishing Your Quilt (page 33) to add the binding.

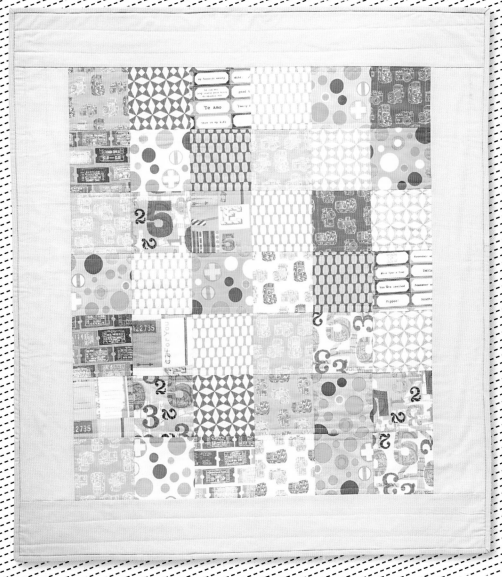

Starter 1 Pretty Flower Pincushion

Everyone who sews needs a pincushion. But not just any pincushion—a pretty one. This project is a great one for leftover 5" × 5" squares, and you'll have a chance to appliqué!

Here's What You Need

- 2 squares 5" × 5"
- Scraps of fabric for appliqué shapes
- 5" × 5" square of fusible fleece
- 5" × 5" square of paper-backed fusible web
- Polyfill or cotton stuffing

Before You Start

- Read through all the instructions before doing any cutting or sewing.

- If you don't know how to do something or you don't remember, go back to that section in the book and find out how.

Here's What to Do

Remember: Seam allowances are ¼".

1. Press the fusible fleece to the *wrong* side of the 5" × 5" square that will be the top of the pincushion. Refer to Using Fusible Fleece (page 26).

2. Copy the Pretty Flower Pincushion flower pattern (page 50) and center pattern (page 51) at 100%. Use the templates to trace 1 flower shape and 1 flower center onto the paper side of the fusible web. Refer to Appliqué (page 27) for instructions on using paper-backed fusible web.

3. Using scissors, cut ¼" outside the lines of each shape.

4. Iron the cut-out shapes onto the *wrong* side of your chosen appliqué fabrics. Remember to follow the instructions that came with the fusible web.

5. Carefully cut out the shapes on the drawn lines.

6. Peel off the paper backing from the flower and center. Center the flower on the right side of the square with the fusible fleece. First press the flower in place. Then do the same with the flower center.

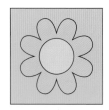

7. Stitch around the edge of the flower and the center. Use a blanket stitch if your machine has it. If not, you can use a zigzag or even a straight stitch.

8. Place the remaining 5″ × 5″ square on top of the appliquéd square, right sides together.

9. Pin together the squares. Stitch around all 4 sides, leaving a 2″ opening on 1 side for turning the pincushion right side out.

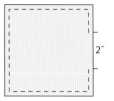

10. Turn the pincushion right side out and stuff it using polyfill or cotton.

11. Pin the opening and hand stitch it closed. If you feel more comfortable, carefully straight stitch the opening closed using your machine.

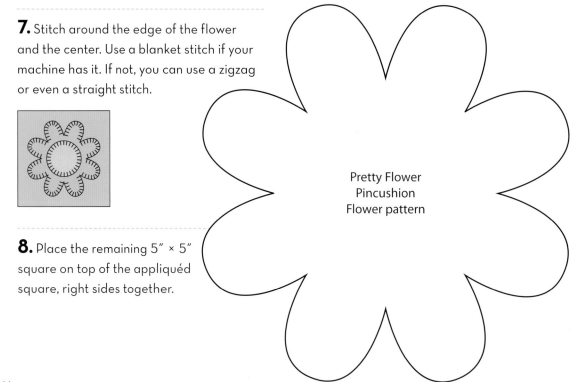

Pretty Flower
Pincushion
Flower pattern

Pretty Flower
Pincushion
Center pattern

2 Next Step Wall Organizer

This project is great for storing all the treasures that seem to go missing in your room. It's perfect for your brush, hair elastics, ribbons, and so on. And don't forget the chargers for your phone and MP3 player. It's a one-stop place to store all your special things so you know right where to look for them.

Here's What You Need

- 15 squares 5″ × 5″
- 1 yard white fabric
- 18½″ × 21½″ piece of fusible fleece
- 24″ length of ½″-diameter dowel

Before You Start

- Read through all the instructions before doing any cutting or sewing.

- If you don't know how to do something or you don't remember, go back to that section in the book and find out how.

Here's What to Do

Remember: Seam allowances are ¼″.

Make the Front of the Organizer

1. Pick 12 of your 5″ × 5″ squares for the wall organizer and 3 squares for the hanging loops.

2. Arrange the 12 squares for the wall organizer into 3 rows of 4 squares each.

3. Stitch together each row. Press the seams.

4. Cut 2 strips 5″ wide across the width of the white fabric. Trim the selvages off at each end. Crosscut the strips so you have 3 strips that are 5″ × 18½″.

5. Place a white backing strip on top of a completed pieced row, right sides together. Stitch around all 4 sides. Leave a 2″ opening on 1 side for turning the piece right side out. Repeat for the remaining 2 strips.

6. Turn all the rows right side out and press well.

7. Cut 2 pieces 18½″ × 21½″ from the white fabric.

8. Press the fusible fleece to the *wrong* side of a white 18½″ × 21½″ piece. Refer to Using Fusible Fleece (page 26).

9. Place the fleece-fused fabric right side up on the table. Along the 21½″ edges of the piece, measure 2″ down from the top, and

pin a charm square strip in place with ¼″ of the white fabric showing on both sides (this will be the seam allowance when you sew the front to the back). Measure and pin the remaining strips on the wallhanging top as shown.

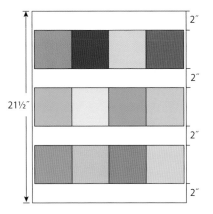

10. Stitch around the 3 edges of each charm square strip as shown. Be sure to catch the open edge as you sew.

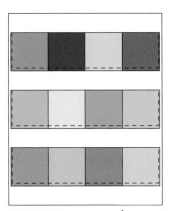

--- *TIP* ----------

Stitching it like this gives you three wide pockets. If you want some smaller pockets, you could stitch in-the-ditch on some of the pieced strips.

Make the Hanging Loops

1. Press each of the 3 remaining 5″ × 5″ squares in half to make a crease. Then open each square with the wrong side facing up so you can see the crease in the strip center.

2. Fold each side in to the center crease. Press.

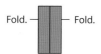

3. Fold the strip in half along the first crease that you made, and press. Stitch along both long sides of the strips. Your 3 hanging loops are ready.

Put Together the Organizer

1. Fold the loops in half, and pin them to the top of the front as shown, aligning the raw edges of the loops with the raw edge of the organizer. Place 1 loop in the center, and 1 loop 1″ in from each outside edge.

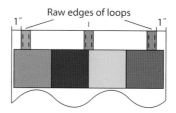

2. Place the other 18½″ × 21½″ white piece so it is right sides together with the organizer front. Pin and carefully stitch around the 4 sides, leaving a 3″ opening on 1 side for turning the organizer right side out.

3. Turn the wall organizer right side out and press. Pin and hand stitch the opening closed.

10" × 10" Squares:

Layer Cakes OR 10" Stackers

1 Starter Sweet Little Pouch

Use up leftover 10" × 10" squares with this quick and easy project. The pouch is perfect for holding all sorts of small things. It's also a great "just because" gift for your BFF.

Here's What You Need

- 2 squares 10" × 10" for outside of pouch

- 1 square 10" × 10" for pocket (Mine matched the outside, though.)

- 2 squares 10" × 10" for lining

- 2 pieces 6½" × 8½" of fusible fleece

- 3" strip of ½"-wide hook-and-loop tape (such as Velcro)

Before You Start

- Read through all the instructions before doing any cutting or sewing.

- If you don't know how to do something or you don't remember, go back to that section in the book and find out how.

Here's What to Do

Remember: Seam allowances are ¼".

Make the Outside of the Pouch

1. Using the 2 outside squares, cut 2 rectangles 6½" × 8½".

2. Fuse the fleece rectangles to the *wrong* sides of both outside 6½" × 8½" pieces. Refer to Using Fusible Fleece (page 26).

3. Cut 2 rectangles 2½" × 8½" from the pocket 10" × 10" square. (Mine matched the front, but it can be a similar or contrasting fabric.)

4. With right sides together, stitch together the pocket 2½" × 8½" rectangles along 1 long edge, leaving the sides and bottom unstitched as shown.

5. Turn the pocket rectangles right side out and press. Pin together the raw edges at the sides and bottom. Stitch ¼" from the top long seam edge of the pocket.

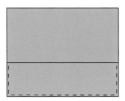

6. Place the pocket on the right side of the outside rectangle, lining up the raw outside edges as shown. Stitch around 3 sides of the pocket close to the raw edges. (The line of stitching from Step 5 does not show in the illustration.)

7. Pin the 2 outside pieces right sides together with the pocket at the bottom between the outside pieces. Stitch around 3 sides, leaving the top open as shown.

Put Together the Pouch

1. Trim the 2 remaining 10" × 10" squares to 6½" × 8½" rectangles for the lining.

2. Fold 1 lining piece in half to find the center along the long edges. Measure 2" down and stitch on 1 side of the hook-and-loop tape. Repeat on the other lining piece to attach the other side of the hook-and-loop tape.

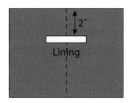

2"
Lining

3. With right sides together, and matching up the hook-and-loop tape, stitch together the 2 lining pieces along 3 sides as shown, leaving a 2" opening on 1 side for turning right side out.

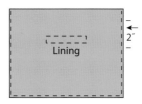

Lining
2"

4. With right sides together, put the outside pouch into the lining, matching up the side seams. Pin the raw edges of the lining and the pouch around the top. Stitch the top edge.

5. Turn the pouch right side out through the opening in the lining. Pin and stitch the opening closed by hand or by machine.

6. Press the top edge of your sweet little pouch and stitch ¼" around the top. Slow down at the side seams to accommodate the extra layers of fabric.

Finished size: 53″ × 53″ • Finished block size: 8¾″ × 8¾″

Fabrics used: Ticklish by Me and My Sister Designs for Moda

Next Step 2 Tropicana Quilt

One of the things that's really fun about this quilt is that you can make it with almost any fabrics. You can pick fabrics to match your bedroom, use your favorite colors, or pick theme colors.

Here's What You Need

- 36 squares 10″ × 10″
- ½ yard fabric for binding
- 3¼ yards fabric for backing
- 57″ × 57″ piece of batting

Before You Start

- Read through all the instructions before doing any cutting or sewing.
- If you don't know how to do something or you don't remember, go back to that section in the book and find out how.

Here's What to Do

Remember: Seam allowances are ¼".

Make the Blocks

There is a really clever way to make the blocks for this quilt. These blocks are sometimes called Hourglass blocks because of the shape.

1. Select 2 of the 10" × 10" squares and place them on top of each other with right sides together. Using a ruler and pencil, draw a diagonal line from corner to corner.

2. Stitch ¼" on both sides of the drawn line.

3. Cut on the drawn line. Open each square. Press the seam toward the darker fabric.

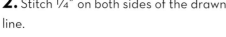

4. On each square from Step 3, use a ruler and pencil to draw a diagonal line from corner to corner as shown. Cut on the drawn line.

Cutting line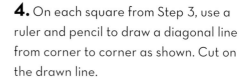

5. Repeat Steps 1–4 with the remaining 10" × 10" squares.

6. Pin and stitch together pairs of triangles. Open the blocks and press the seam allowances. Repeat this step until you have 36 blocks. Refer to Cool Trick! Nesting Seams (page 25) to help you make the blocks.

7. Trim the blocks to remove the little dog-ear triangles that extend beyond the edges of the blocks.

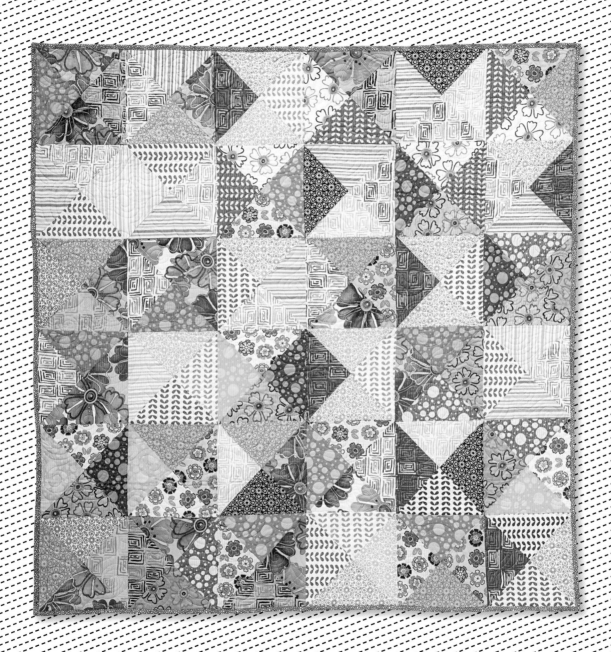

You can pick fabrics to match your bedroom, use your favorite colors, or pick theme colors.

Put Together the Quilt

1. Look at the quilt photo (page 65) and the quilt diagram to arrange the blocks into 6 rows with 6 blocks in each row. Play with the placement until you like the way it looks. Pay attention to how the blocks are turned. It makes a difference in how they look. To keep your blocks in order, refer to Cool Trick! Numbering Your Blocks (page 24) and label your blocks.

2. Stitch the blocks into rows. Refer to Cool Trick! Nesting Seams (page 25) and press the odd-row seams to the right and the even-row seams to the left.

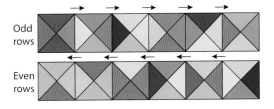

Odd rows

Even rows

3. Stitch together the rows to complete the quilt top. Give the top a good pressing to make sure all the seams are flat and smooth.

4. Cut and piece the backing to 57″ × 57″.

5. Assemble your quilt sandwich, baste, and quilt. Refer to Turning a Quilt Top into a Quilt (page 29). I used straight-line quilting on my quilt.

6. Cut 6 strips 2½″ wide across the width of the binding fabric. Refer to Finishing Your Quilt (page 33) to complete the binding.

2 Next Step Love Hearts Pillow

There is nothing nicer than snuggling up with a good book and a comfy pillow on a gloomy day!

This project is great for leftover 10" × 10" squares. Pick some darling prints and get sewing!

Here's What You Need

- 4 squares 10" × 10"
- ½ yard fabric for pillow back
- 2 scraps for appliqué hearts, each at least 7" × 8"
- ¼ yard paper-backed fusible web
- 16½" × 16½" square of fusible fleece
- 14" × 14" pillow insert (from a fabric or craft store)

Before You Start

- Read through all the instructions before doing any cutting or sewing.
- If you don't know how to do something or you don't remember, go back to that section in the book and find out how.

Here's What to Do

Remember: Seam allowances are ¼".

Make the Pillow Top

1. Copy the Love Hearts Pillow pattern (page 72) at 100%. Use the template to trace 2 hearts onto the paper side of the fusible web. Refer to Appliqué (page 27) for instructions on using paper-backed fusible web.

2. Using scissors, cut ¼" outside the lines of each shape.

3. Iron the cut-out shapes onto the *wrong* side of your chosen appliqué fabrics. Remember to follow the instructions that came with the fusible web.

4. Carefully cut out the shapes on the drawn lines.

5. Trim the 10″ × 10″ squares down to 8½″ × 8½″ squares.

6. Plan the arrangement of the squares. With right sides together, pin and sew together 2 of the 8½″ × 8½″ squares. Repeat with the remaining 2 squares. Refer to Cool Trick! Nesting Seams (page 25), and press the top-row seam to the right and the bottom-row seam to the left.

7. Pin and stitch together the 2 block units to make a 4-block pillow top. Press the seam.

8. Look at the pillow photo (page 71). Place the 2 heart shapes on your pillow top. When you are happy with how they look, peel off the paper backing and fuse them to the pillow top, following the manufacturer's instructions.

9. Stitch around the hearts. Use a blanket stitch if your machine has it. If not, you can use a zigzag or even a straight stitch.

10. Refer to Using Fusible Fleece (page 26) to fuse the 16½″ × 16½″ square of fusible fleece to the *wrong* side of the pillow top.

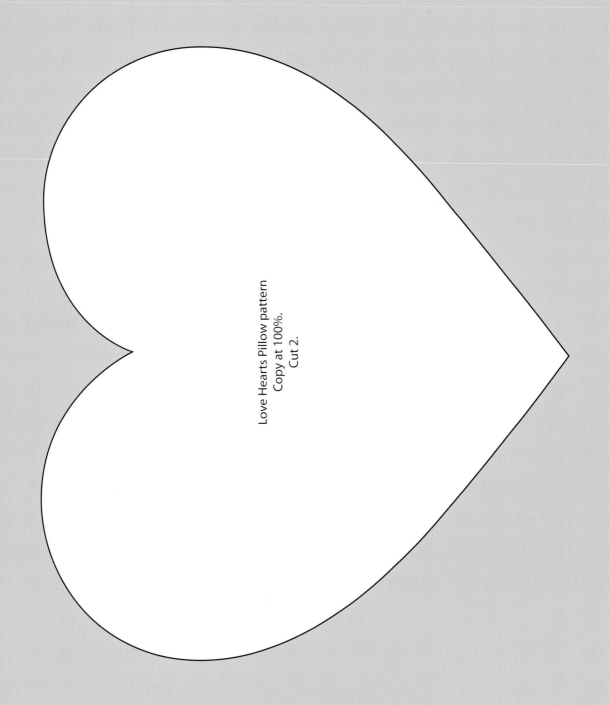

Love Hearts Pillow pattern
Copy at 100%.
Cut 2.

Put Together the Pillow

1. From the pillow back fabric, cut
1 square 16½" × 16½" and 1 rectangle
8½" × 16½".

2. Zigzag stitch on an edge of the
16½" × 16½" square, covering the raw
edge. Measure 2" in from the zigzagged
edge, fold with wrong sides together, and
press. Stitch close to the zigzagged edge
as shown.

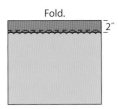

Fold.

2"

3. Zigzag stitch a long edge of the
8½" × 16½" piece. Measure 1" from the
zigzagged edge, fold with wrong sides
together, and press. Stitch close to the
zigzagged edge as shown.

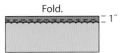

Fold.

1"

4. Place the pillow top with the right side
facing *up*. Place the piece from Step 3 on
the pillow top, right side *down* as shown.

5. Place the piece from Step 2 right side
facing down also, so it overlaps with the
smaller backing piece. Pin in place. Stitch
around all 4 sides. Turn the pillow right side
out and press. Put the pillow insert inside.

Next Step 2 Snowballs Quilt

Can you believe it? Snowball. That's the name of this quilt block. With so many fun packs of 10" × 10" squares, you'll have lots of fabrics to choose from.

Here's What You Need

- 30 squares 10" × 10"
- 1⅞ yards white fabric for blocks and binding
- 3 yards fabric for backing
- 52" × 62" piece of batting

Before You Start

- Read through all the instructions before doing any cutting or sewing.

- If you don't know how to do something or you don't remember, go back to that section in the book and find out how.

Here's What to Do

Remember: Seam allowances are ¼".

Make the Blocks

1. Refer to Cutting Fabric (page 20). From the white fabric, cut 12 strips 3½" wide across the fabric. Crosscut into 3½" × 3½" squares. You'll need 120.

2. Using a ruler and pencil, draw a diagonal line from corner to corner on the wrong side of each white 3½" × 3½" square.

3. Place 4 white squares, right sides together, on the corners of a 10" × 10" square. Notice the direction of the drawn lines! Pin the white squares in place.

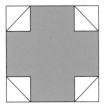

4. Stitch on the drawn lines of the white squares.

5. Trim off the excess fabric, leaving a ¼" seam as shown. Press the corners open.

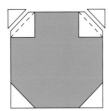

6. Repeat Steps 3–5 until you have made 30 Snowball blocks.

Put Together the Quilt

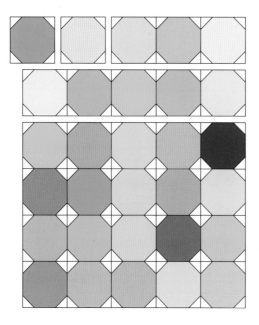

1. Look at the quilt photo (page 77) and the quilt diagram to arrange the blocks into 6 rows with 5 blocks in each row. Play with the placement until you like the way it looks. To keep your blocks in order, refer to Cool Trick! Numbering Your Blocks (page 24) and label your blocks.

2. Stitch the blocks into rows. Refer to Cool Trick! Nesting Seams (page 25), and press the odd-row seams to the right and the even-row seams to the left.

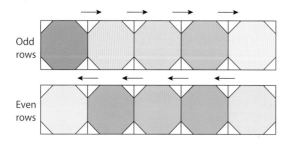

Odd rows

Even rows

3. Stitch together the rows to complete the quilt top. Give the top a good pressing to make sure all the seams are flat and smooth.

4. Cut and piece the backing to be 52″ × 62″.

5. Assemble your quilt sandwich, baste, and quilt. Refer to Turning a Quilt Top into a Quilt (page 29). I quilted mine with a free-motion swirl design.

6. Cut 6 strips 2½″ wide across the width of the binding fabric. Refer to Finishing Your Quilt (page 33) to complete the binding.

2½" Strips

Jelly Rolls, Rolie Polies, OR Bali Pops

Finished size: 48½″ × 48½″ • Finished block size: 8″ × 8″

Fabrics used: Comma by Zen Chic for Moda

Starter 1 Concrete Jungle Quilt

This is a great project to work on. You can practice your sewing and quilting skills and have a few strips left over for other projects.

Here's What You Need

- 36 strips of 2½″-wide print
- ¾ yard gray solid
- ⅝ yard fabric for binding
- 3 yards fabric for backing
- 53″ × 53″ piece of batting

Before You Start

- Read through all the instructions before doing any cutting or sewing.
- If you don't know how to do something or you don't remember, go back to that section in the book and find out how.

Here's What to Do

Remember: Seam allowances are ¼".

Cut the Fabric

Refer to Cutting Fabric (page 20).

1. Choose 36 strips from the roll.

2. From each strip, cut:

    1 square 2½" × 2½"

    2 rectangles 2½" × 4½"

    2 rectangles 2½" × 8½"

3. From the gray solid fabric, cut 14 strips 1½" wide across the width of the fabric. Crosscut:

    72 rectangles 1½" × 2½"

    72 rectangles 1½" × 4½"

Make the Blocks

1. Stitch 1½" × 2½" gray rectangles to opposite sides of a 2½" × 2½" print square as shown. Press the seams toward the gray.

2. Stitch 1½" × 4½" gray rectangles to the top and bottom of the block. Press the seams toward the gray.

3. Stitch matching 2½" × 4½" print rectangles to both sides of the block. Press toward the print.

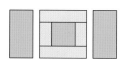 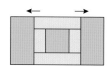

4. Stitch matching 2½″ × 8½″ print rectangles to the top and bottom of the block. Press toward the print.

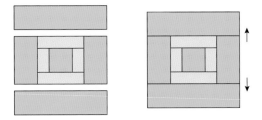

5. Repeat Steps 1–4 until you have a total of 36 blocks.

Put Together the Quilt

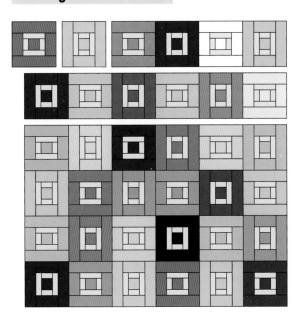

1. Look at the quilt diagram to arrange the blocks into 6 rows with 6 blocks in each row. Play with the placement until you like the way it looks. Pay attention to the direction of the seams in each block in the rows, and notice that the seams alternate directions in the diagram. The blocks will be much easier to sew and press with the seams like this. I wish I had done it on my quilt!

2. To keep your blocks in order once you have all the blocks arranged and turned correctly, refer to Cool Trick! Numbering Your Blocks (page 24) and label your blocks.

3. Stitch the blocks into rows. Refer to Cool Trick! Nesting Seams (page 25) and press all the seams. Press the odd-row seams to the right and the even-row seams to the left.

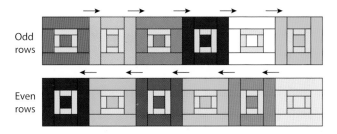

Odd rows

Even rows

4. Stitch together the rows to complete the quilt top. Give the top a good pressing to make sure all the seams are flat and smooth.

5. Cut and piece the backing fabric to be 53″ × 53″.

6. Assemble your quilt sandwich, baste, and quilt. Refer to Turning a Quilt Top into a Quilt (page 29). I quilted mine with a free-motion wavy line design.

7. Cut 6 strips 2½″ wide across the width of the binding fabric. Refer to Finishing Your Quilt (page 33) to add the binding.

I Can Sing a Rainbow Quilt

1

Starter

Don't you just love all these bright colors? When you pick your precut roll for this quilt, look for one that has at least three strips of each color but in different patterns. If you like the quilt block but don't want the rainbow look, have fun picking out other colors.

Here's What You Need

- 30 strips of 2½"-wide print
- 1½ yards white fabric
- 3 yards fabric for backing
- 52" × 69" piece of batting

Before You Start

- Read through all the instructions before doing any cutting or sewing.

- If you don't know how to do something or you don't remember, go back to that section in the book and find out how.

Here's What to Do

Remember: Seam allowances are ¼".

Make the Blocks

1. Choose 24 strips for the blocks and 6 strips for the binding. Set aside the binding strips.

2. Place the strips for the blocks into groups of 3. You will have a total of 8 groups. Look at the quilt photo to see how the colors are grouped together. You may want to group your strips by colors or patterns. Play with them until you like the groups.

3. Stitch together each group of 3 strips. These are called *strip sets*. Press the seam allowances all in the same direction. Trim the ends of each strip set so they are even.

Strip Set

Strips of fabric that are sewn together and then crosscut.

4. Cut each strip set into 8" pieces. You will have 5 pieces from each strip set.

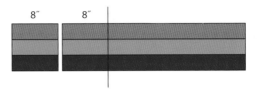

5. From the white fabric, cut 34 strips 1½" wide across the width of the fabric. Trim off the selvages on the strips. Crosscut the strips into:

80 strips 1½" × 6½"

80 strips 1½" × 10"

6. Stitch white 1½" × 6½" strips to both ends of each 8" strip set section. Press the seams *away* from the white fabric.

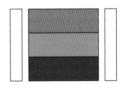 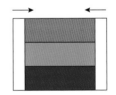

7. Stitch white 1½" × 10" strips to the top and bottom of each 8" strip set section. Press the seams *away* from the white fabric.

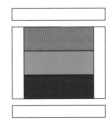 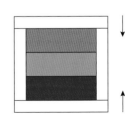

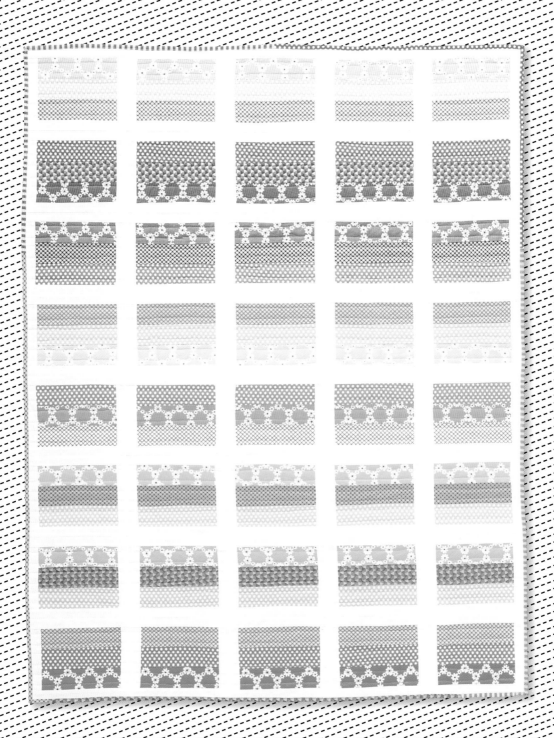

Put Together the Quilt

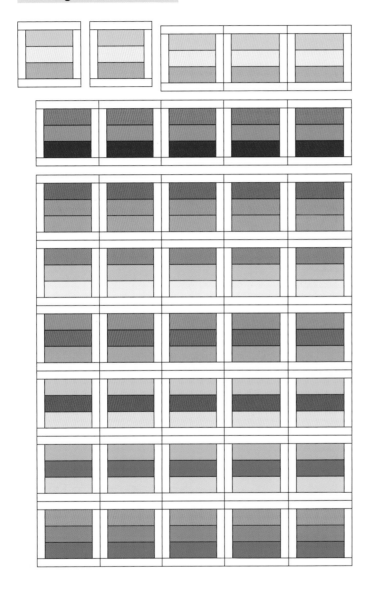

1. Look at the quilt photo (page 89) and the quilt diagram (page 90) to arrange the blocks into 8 rows with 5 blocks in each row. The quilt in the photo has the blocks in color order, but you might want a different arrangement. Play with the placement until you like the way it looks. To keep your blocks in order, refer to Cool Trick! Numbering Your Blocks (page 24) and label your blocks.

2. Stitch the blocks into rows. Refer to Cool Trick! Nesting Seams (page 25) and press all the seams. Press the odd-row seams to the right and the even-row seams to the left.

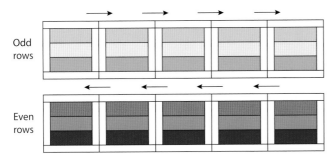

3. Stitch together the rows to complete the quilt top. Give the top a good pressing to make sure all the seams are flat and smooth.

4. Cut and piece the backing fabric to be 52″ × 68″.

5. Assemble your quilt sandwich, baste, and quilt. Refer to Turning a Quilt Top into a Quilt (page 29). My quilt has straight-line quilting. Line up your walking foot along the seam as a guide. This is a very easy and doable way of quilting your quilts.

6. Use the 6 strips you set aside to add the binding. Refer to Finishing Your Quilt (page 33).

1 Starter

Striped Pillow

How cute is this pillow? It's a great project to make out of leftover 2½" strips. Why not make two or three and stack them up on your bed?

Here's What You Need

- 4–7 strips 2½" × 40", depending on how many colors you want
- ½ yard fabric for pillow back
- 12" × 18" pillow insert (from a fabric or craft store)

Before You Start

- Read through all the instructions before doing any cutting or sewing.
- If you don't know how to do something or you don't remember, go back to that section in the book and find out how.

TIP

Before you start cutting, look at your precut strips and think about which ones you want to use. Some rolls of precut strips have duplicate fabrics, but others don't. If you want to make a pillow like the one pictured, you'll need 2 strips 40" long of 2 colors (you can get 2 cut 19" pieces per 40" strip). But don't worry—this pillow would be just as fun using a different color for each stripe. The number of strips you need will depend on whether or not you are using the same fabric for more than 1 stripe.

Here's What to Do

Remember: Seam allowances are ¼".

1. Refer to Cutting Fabric (page 20). Cut the 2½"-wide strips so you have 7 pieces 19" long. (The number of 2½" × 40" strips you need will depend on whether or not you are using the same fabric for more than 1 stripe.)

2. Make a pleasing arrangement with your strips. Pin together and then stitch the 7 strips to make the pillow top. Press the seams all in the same direction.

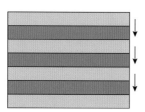

3. To cover the raw edge, zigzag stitch a short edge of the pillow top. Fold the zigzagged edge ½" to the wrong side and press. Stitch close to the zigzagged edge.

Fold ½".

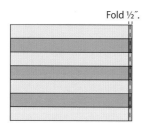

4. Cut the piece of backing fabric to 13" × 24".

5. Zigzag stitch a short side of the backing 13" × 24" piece. Fold the zigzagged edge over ½" to the wrong side and press. Stitch close to the zigzagged edge, like you did on the pillow top.

6. Measure 5" from the folded edge of the back, and fold the fabric to the wrong side to create a flap along the 5" line. Press. Do not stitch this after folding. (Stitching from Step 5 does not show in the diagram.)

Fold 5".

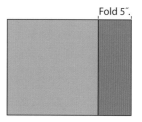

7. Place the backing piece and the pieced pillow front right sides together. Pin around 3 sides. Stitch around the 3 sides. Secure the seams with *backstitching* at the folded edges.

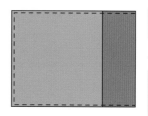

---DEFINITION---
Backstitching
Stitching backward for a few stitches to keep a seam from coming unstitched.

8. Turn the pillow right side out, place the pillow insert inside, and fold the flap over the insert to tuck the pillow in place.

2 Next Step Accessories Pouch

This is a great little pouch to keep your phone, MP3 player, head-phones, jewelry, or any of those little things that you're always losing. You can throw the pouch in your purse or bag and keep all those little things together.

Here's What You Need

- 2 strips 2½" wide of different colors for outside of pouch
- 1 fat quarter for lining
- 2 pieces 5½" × 6½" of fusible fleece
- 3" piece of ½"-wide hook-and-loop tape (such as Velcro)

Before You Start

- Read through all the instructions before doing any cutting or sewing.
- If you don't know how to do something or you don't remember, go back to that section in the book and find out how.

Here's What to Do

Remember: Seam allowances are ¼".

Make the Outside of the Pouch

1. Decide which strip you want to be the pouch flap and center strip. Refer to Cutting Fabric (page 20). From this strip, cut 2 pieces 2½" × 5½". Then cut the remaining length of the strip so that it is 1½" wide and set this narrow strip aside.

2. Cut the strip that you want for the sides of the pouch in half so you have 2 pieces, each 2½" × 20".

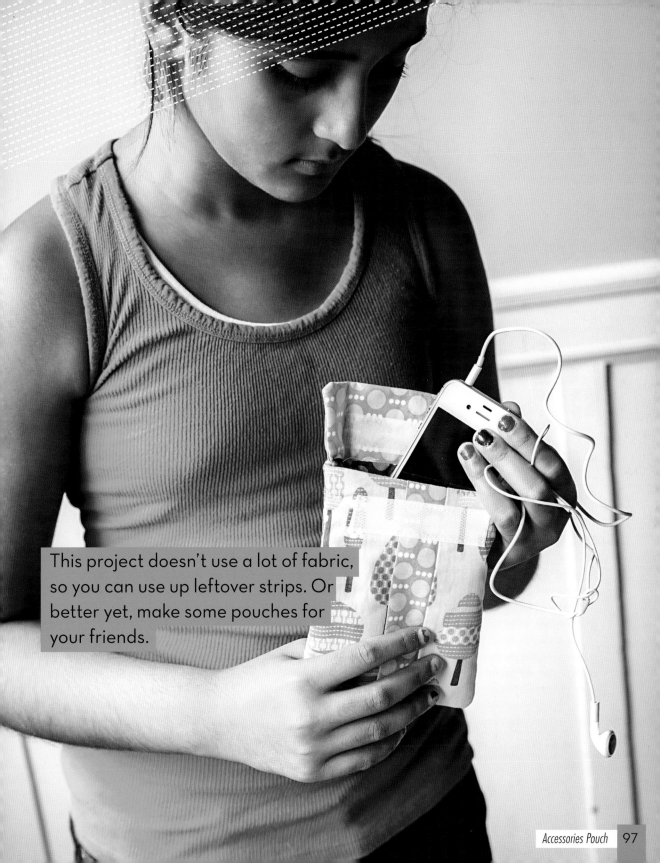

This project doesn't use a lot of fabric, so you can use up leftover strips. Or better yet, make some pouches for your friends.

3. Stitch the 1½" strip from Step 1 between the 2½" × 20" strips as shown. This is a *strip set*. Press the seams toward the darker fabric. Trim the ends of the strip set so they are even.

--- DEFINITION ---

Strip Set

Strips of fabric that are sewn together and then crosscut.

4. Cut 2 sections 6½" long from the strip set as shown. These are the front and back pieces for the outside of the pouch.

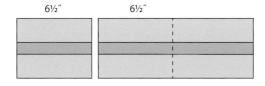

6½"   6½"

5. Press a piece of fusible fleece to the *wrong* sides of both pieces from Step 4. Refer to Using Fusible Fleece (page 26).

6. Fold 1 of the fused pieces in half lengthwise and use your fingers to press a crease in the center of the center strip as shown. This will be the front of your pouch.

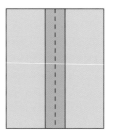

7. On the front piece, measure down 1½" from the top along the crease. Pin and stitch 1 of the hook-and-loop pieces to the right side of the fabric.

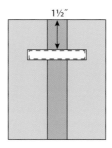

1½"

8. Place the front and back pouch pieces right sides together. Stitch around 3 sides, leaving the edges nearest the hook-and-loop tape open. Turn the pouch right side out.

Fleece

Make the Flap

1. Finger-press the center of 1 of the 2½" × 5½" strips and then measure ¾" from the bottom. Pin and stitch the remaining piece of hook-and-loop tape to the right side of the strip.

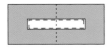

2. With right sides together, pin together the 2½" × 5½" pieces. Stitch around 3 sides. Turn right side out. This is the flap.

Put Together the Pouch

1. With the nontape side of the flap against the right side of the pouch back, pin and stitch the flap to the top of the pouch back, matching the center of the flap with the center of the back.

Raw edges

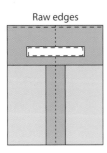

2. Cut 2 rectangles 5½" × 6½" from the lining fabric. Put the 2 pieces right sides together and stitch around 3 sides, leaving a 2" opening as shown on 1 side for turning the pouch right side out.

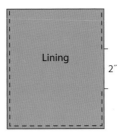

Lining

2"

3. With right sides together, put the pouch into the lining, matching the side seams. Pin the top raw edges together. Stitch around the top, slowing down at the side seams to accommodate the extra layers of fabric. Turn the pouch right side out through the opening in the lining.

4. Press around the top edge of your pouch. Pin and stitch the opening closed by hand or by machine.

Fat Quarters

Sleepover Set—Pillowcase

Starter 1

Make a pillowcase so you can take your favorite pillow with you on sleepovers. Coordinate it with your Essentials Bag (page 106), or not.

Here's What You Need

- 6 fat quarters
- ¾ yard fabric for backing

Before You Start

- Read through all the instructions before doing any cutting or sewing.
- If you don't know how to do something or you don't remember, go back to that section in the book and find out how.

Here's What to Do

Remember: Seam allowances are ¼".

1. Refer to Cutting Fabric (page 20). Cut a 5½" × 22" strip from each of the 6 fat quarters.

2. Place the 6 strips on a table. Move the strips around until you like the arrangement.

3. Place the first 2 strips right sides together. Pin them together and then stitch. Sew together the rest of the strips in the same way. This is the pillow front.

4. On a short end of the pillow top, zigzag stitch over the raw edge. Fold the zigzagged edge ½" to the wrong side and press. Stitch close to the zigzagged edge.

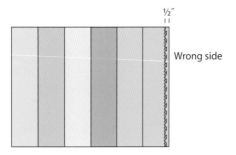

½"

Wrong side

5. Cut a 22"-wide strip across the width of the pillow backing fabric. Trim it to 22" × 36".

6. Use a zigzag stitch to cover the raw edge along a 22" end of the backing. Fold the zigzagged edge ½" to the wrong side and press. Stitch close to the zigzagged edge like you did on the pillow front.

7. Measure 6" from the folded edge of the backing piece. Fold along the 6" line with wrong sides together, and press. Do not stitch this after folding. (Stitching from Step 6 does not show in the diagram.)

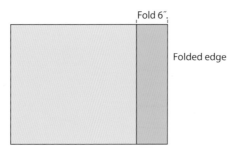

Fold 6".

Folded edge

8. Place the backing piece and the pieced pillow front right sides together, matching up the folded edges. Slightly trim the outside raw-edged sides to be even if they don't match exactly. Pin and stitch around the 3 raw-edged sides as shown. Secure the seams with *backstitching* at the folded edges.

Folded edges

9. Turn the pillowcase right side out and press. It's ready to hold your favorite pillow. Use the backing flap to tuck around your pillow.

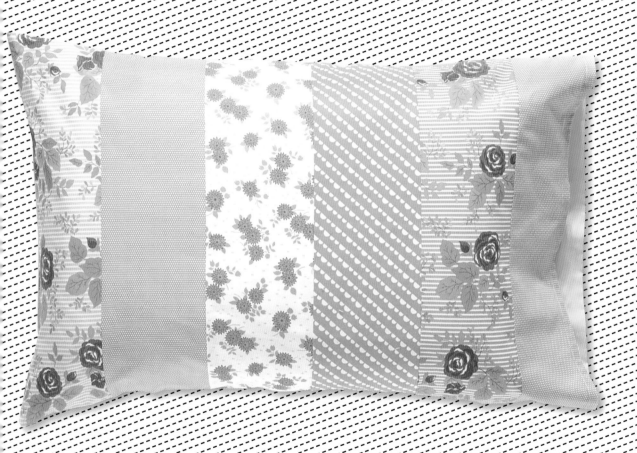

Sleepover Set—Essentials Bag

Finished size: 16" × 16"

Fabrics used: Happy Go Lucky by Bonnie and Camille for Moda

Use Your Skills **3**

Off to a sleepover with your friends? Here's a bag to take your pajamas and all your essentials. Pair it with a pillowcase (page 102) and you're all set.

Pair it with a pillowcase (page 102)

Here's What You Need

- 2 fat quarters for outside of bag
- 2 fat quarters for lining
- 1 fat quarter for pocket
- ⅓ yard fabric for handle
- 2 squares 16½" × 16½" of fusible fleece

Before You Start

- Read through all the instructions before doing any cutting or sewing.
- If you don't know how to do something or you don't remember, go back to that section in the book and find out how.

Here's What to Do

Remember: Seam allowances are ¼".

Make the Outside of the Bag

1. Refer to Cutting Fabric (page 20). From the 2 fat quarters for the outside of the bag, cut 2 squares 16½" × 16½".

2. Press the 16½" × 16½" squares of fusible fleece to the *wrong* sides of the outside bag fabric 16½" × 16½" squares. Refer to Using Fusible Fleece (page 26).

3. Cut the fat quarter for the pocket into 2 rectangles, each 6½" × 14½".

4. Place the 2 pocket pieces right sides together. Stitch around all 4 sides, leaving a 2" opening on 1 side for turning the pocket right side out.

5. Turn the pocket right side out through the 2" opening. Stitch ¼" from the top edge as shown.

6. Fold the pocket in half to find the middle of the pocket length and use your fingers to press a crease in the middle. Then fold 1 fused square in half and finger-press a crease in the middle.

7. Measure 2½" from the bottom. With the stitched pocket edge toward the top, pin the pocket to the right side of the square, 2½" above the bottom edge of the square, matching the center creases. Stitch around 3 sides of the pocket, leaving the top of the pocket open. *Backstitch* when you start and

stop stitching. Be sure to catch the pocket opening (where you turned the pocket) in the stitching. (The stitching from Step 5 does not show in the illustration.)

---DEFINITION---

Backstitching

Stitching back-ward for a few stitches to keep a seam from coming unstitched.

--- TIP ----------

This makes one big outside pocket, but you may want to stitch on the pocket center foldline to make two small outside pockets.

8. Place the 2 outside bag pieces right sides together, keeping the pocket to the bottom of the bag. Stitch around 3 sides, leaving the top open. Backstitch when you start and stop stitching.

9. Give the bag sides and corners some shape with the technique in Cool Trick! Boxed Corners (below). Use this trick on the bottom corners of the bag.

--- COOL TRICK! ---

Boxed Corners

A With the bag still right sides together, at 1 corner match the side seam exactly with the bottom seam to create a point, and pin in place.

B Mark 1" down on each side from the point. Draw a line between the dots.

Ruler

C Stitch across the line. Backstitch when you start and stop stitching.

D Trim off the excess, leaving a 1/4" seam allowance.

E Finish the other corner of the bag. Then turn the bag right side out and see your boxed corners!

Make the Straps

1. Cut a 5"-wide strip across the width of the handle fabric. Trim the selvages off at each end. Cut the strip in half so you have 2 strips, each about 20" long.

2. Press the handle strips in half lengthwise with wrong sides together. Open the strips flat with the wrong side up so that you can see a creased line down the center of the strip.

3. Fold each side in to the center crease. Press.

4. Fold the strips in half along the first crease that you made, and press. Stitch along both long sides of each strip.

Put Together the Bag

1. On the top edge, find the centers of the front and back pieces as shown. Measure 3″ in both directions from the centers on the front and the back as shown. Pin and stitch 1 handle strip to the front and the other handle strip to the back of the bag. Make sure that the raw edges of the handles match the raw edges of the top of the bag. Be careful not to get any twists in the handles.

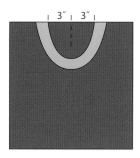

2. From the 2 fat quarters for the lining, cut 2 squares 16½″ × 16½″.

3. Place the 2 lining pieces right sides together. Stitch around 3 sides, leaving a 3″ opening in 1 side for turning the bag right side out. Backstitch when you start and stop stitching. Leave the top open.

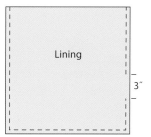

4. Make the bottom corners in the lining the same as you did for the outside of the bag, but do not turn the lining right side out when you finish the corners. Refer to Cool Trick! Boxed Corners (page 110).

5. With right sides together, put the outside of the bag into the lining, matching up the side seams. Pin the top raw edges together. Stitch around the top, slowing down at the side seams to accommodate the extra layers of fabric. Turn the bag right side out through the opening in the lining.

6. Press around the top edge of the bag. Then stitch ¼″ from the edge around the top of the bag. Pin and stitch the opening in the lining closed by hand or by machine.

2 Next Step Shooting Stars Pencil Roll

Here's a great way to keep all your pens and pencils together.

Here's What You Need

- 1 fat quarter of star fabric
- 1 fat quarter of red chevron fabric
- 8½" × 13" piece of fusible fleece
- 18" of ½"-wide ribbon

Before You Start

- Read through all the instructions before doing any cutting or sewing.

- If you don't know how to do something or you don't remember, go back to that section in the book and find out how.

Here's What to Do

Remember: Seam allowances are ¼".

1. From the red chevron fabric, cut 2 rectangles 5½" × 13".

2. Place the chevron 5½" × 13" rectangles with right sides together. Pin together and stitch only across 1 long side.

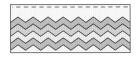

3. Open up the chevron rectangle. Press the seam along the top edge.

4. From the star fabric, cut 2 rectangles 8½" × 13".

5. Press the fusible fleece to the *wrong* side of 1 of the star 8½" × 13" rectangles. Refer to Using Fusible Fleece (page 26).

6. Place the red chevron rectangle on the fused star rectangle, matching the outside raw edges as shown. Pin in place.

7. On the chevron fabric, measure in ½" from the left and right raw edges. Using a ruler and pencil, draw a line from the top of the chevron piece to the bottom on each side. Then, between those lines, measure and mark 11 lines 1" apart across the chevron fabric to form 12 pencil pockets.

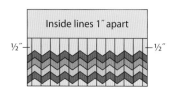

8. Carefully stitch from the top of the chevron fabric to the bottom along each of the marked lines. *Backstitch* at the top edge of each line. These are the pockets for your pens and pencils.

--DEFINITION-----

Backstitching
Stitching backward for a few stitches to keep a seam from coming unstitched.

9. Place the remaining star 8½" × 13" rectangle on top of the pencil roll with the fabrics right sides together. Pin all the edges together. Stitch around the 4 sides, leaving a 3" opening along 1 side for turning the pencil roll right side out.

10. Turn your pencil roll right side out through the side opening. Pin the opening closed. Stitch around the 4 sides close to the edge. Make sure to catch the open side seam in the stitching. When you roll up your pencils, use the ribbon to tie around your pencil roll.

Use Your Skills 3

Day Trip Messenger Bag

Finished size: 12″ × 12″

Fabrics used: Little Matryoshka by Riley Blake Designs

Heading out for the day? This bag is perfect for you! A long strap means it's super comfy, and a secure flap keeps everything inside (where it belongs).

Here's What You Need

- 2 fat quarters for outside of bag
- 2 fat quarters for lining
- 1 fat quarter for flap
- 1⁄3 yard fabric for strap
- 3″ piece of 1⁄2″-wide hook-and-loop tape (such as Velcro)
- 2 squares 12½″ × 12½″ of fusible fleece
- 1 rectangle 8½″ × 12½″ of fusible fleece

Before You Start

- Read through all the instructions before doing any cutting or sewing.
- If you don't know how to do something or you don't remember, go back to that section in the book and find out how.

Here's What to Do

Remember: Seam allowances are ¼".

Make the Outside of the Bag

COOL TIP!

Directional Fabric

Sometimes the print of fabric has a specific direction, like the flap on this messenger bag. You wouldn't want the dolls upside down! You should always decide whether or not it will matter which way the fabric print goes in your project and then cut the fabric accordingly.

1. Refer to Cutting Fabric (page 20). Cut 2 squares 12½" × 12½" from the fat quarters for the outside of the body of the bag (not the flap).

2. Press a 12½" × 12½" square of fusible fleece to the *wrong* side of each 12½" × 12½" square. Refer to Using Fusible Fleece (page 26).

3. Fold 1 of the outside bag squares in half to find the center. Measure 6" from the bottom. Pin and stitch on 1 side of the hook-and-loop tape as shown.

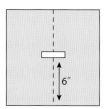

4. Place the 2 outside bag squares with right sides together. Stitch around 3 sides, leaving the top open as shown. Backstitch when you start and stop stitching.

Fleece

5. Refer to Cool Trick! Boxed Corners (page 110) to flatten out the bottom corners of the bag. Measure in 1". Draw a line. Stitch along the line. Trim off the excess. This gives shape to the bottom and sides of the bag.

Make the Flap

1. Cut 2 rectangles 8½″ × 12½″ from the fat quarter for the flap.

2. Press the 8½″ × 12½″ rectangle of fusible fleece to the *wrong* side of 1 of the flap 8½″ × 12½″ rectangles. Refer to Using Fusible Fleece (page 26).

3. Fold the flap rectangle with the fleece in half to find the center. Measure 1½″ from the bottom. Pin and stitch on the other side of the hook-and-loop tape as shown.

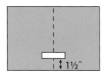

4. Place the 2 flap rectangles with right sides together as shown. Stitch around 3 sides, leaving the top open.

5. Turn the flap right side out and stitch around the 3 stitched sides ¼″ from the edge.

Make the Strap

1. Refer to Cutting Fabric (page 20). Cut a 5″-wide strip across the width of the strap fabric (the strip should be about 40″ long). Trim the selvages off at each end.

2. Press the strip in half lengthwise with wrong sides together. Open the strip flat with the wrong side up so that you can see a creased line down the center of the strip.

3. Fold each side in to the center crease. Press.

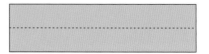

4. Fold the strip in half along the first crease that you made, and press. Stitch along both long sides of the strip.

Put Together the Bag

1. With the flap side without the tape against the right side of the bag back, pin the flap to the back of the bag. Make sure the raw edges of the flap match up with the raw edge of the bag. Stitch the flap to the back across the top edge. (The stitching on the flap does not show in the diagram.)

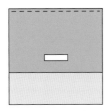

2. Center each end of the strap on a side seam of the outside of the bag. Make sure the raw edges are matched up. Pin and stitch each end of the strap. Be sure that the strap is not twisted!

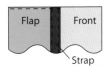

3. Cut 2 squares 12½" × 12½" from the lining fat quarters.

4. Place the lining squares right sides together. Stitch around 3 sides, leaving a 3" opening on 1 side for turning the bag right side out. Backstitch when you start and stop stitching.

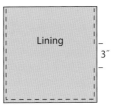

5. Make the corners in the lining the same as you did for the outside of the bag, but do not turn the lining right side out when you finish the corners. Refer to Cool Trick! Boxed Corners (page 110).

6. With right sides together, place the bag into the lining, matching the side seams. Pin the top raw edges together. Stitch ¼" from the edge around the top of the bag, slowing down at the side seams to accommodate the extra layers of fabric. Turn the bag right side out through the opening in the lining.

7. Press around the top edge of the bag. Stitch ¼" from the edge around the top of the bag. Pin and stitch the opening in the lining closed by hand or by machine.

Finished size: 14" × 14"

Fabrics used: Indie Chic by Riley Blake Designs

Use Your Skills 3 Indie Sling Bag

Here's a sling-style bag you can use for school or fun. A large-print fabric makes this bag a standout!

Before You Start

- Read through all the instructions before doing any cutting or sewing.
- If you don't know how to do something or you don't remember, go back to that section in the book and find out how.

Remember: Seam allowances are ¼".

Make the Outside of the Bag

1. Refer to Cutting Fabric (page 20). Cut 2 squares 14½" × 14½" from the fat quarters for the outside of the bag.

2. Press the fusible fleece squares to the *wrong* sides of the 14½" × 14½" squares for the outside of the bag. Refer to Using Fusible Fleece (page 26).

3. Place the 2 outside bag pieces right sides together. Pin and stitch around 3 sides. Backstitch when you start and stop stitching. Leave the top open.

Fleece

4. Refer to Cool Trick! Boxed Corners (page 110) to flatten out the bottom corners of the bag. Measure in 1". Draw a line. Stitch along the line. Trim off the excess. This gives shape to the bottom and sides of the bag.

5. Turn the bag right side out.

Make the Strap

1. From the coordinating fabric for the strap, cut 1 strip 5" wide across the width of the fabric (the strip should be about 40" long). Trim the selvages off at each end. Refer to Cutting Fabric (page 20).

2. Press the handle strip in half lengthwise with wrong sides together. Open the strip flat with the wrong side up so that you can see a creased line down the center of the strip.

3. Fold each side in to the center crease. Press.

4. Fold the strip in half along the first crease that you made, and press. Stitch along both long sides of the strip.

Put Together the Bag

1. Center each end of the strap on a side seam of the outside of the bag. Make sure the raw edges are matched up. Pin and stitch each end of the strap. Be sure that the strap is not twisted!

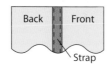

2. Place the 2 lining pieces right sides together. Pin and stitch around 3 sides, leaving a 3″ opening along 1 side for turning the bag right side out. Backstitch when you start and stop stitching.

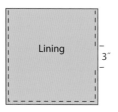

3. Make the bottom corners in the lining the same as you did for the outside of the bag, but do not turn the lining right side out when you finish the corners. Refer to Cool Trick! Boxed Corners (page 110).

4. Put the outside of the bag into the lining with right sides together, matching the side seams. Pin the top raw edges together. Stitch around the top. Turn the bag right side out through the opening in the lining.

5. Press around the top edge of the bag. Stitch ¼″ from the edge around the top of the bag. Pin and stitch the opening in the lining closed by hand or by machine.

Resources

The tools and supplies needed for the projects in this book are generally available in fabric, quilt, and craft stores.

Fabric manufacturers have websites where you can view their fabrics and find retail outlets.

The fabrics used in this book were made by the following companies:

Michael Miller Fabrics
michaelmillerfabrics.com

Moda Fabrics
unitednotions.com

Riley Blake Designs
rileyblakedesigns.com

Robert Kaufman Fabrics
robertkaufman.com

For cut-resistant gloves to use when rotary cutting:

Performance Shield Cut Resistant Glove in X-small
victorinox.com

Sewing machine and machine accessories courtesy of Husqvarna Viking

husqvarnaviking.com